I0555021

gathering

shadows

it started with us – A Poem

tender tulip

It begins with us

Paperback ISBN: 978-1-961902-07-7

Printed in the United States of America

Cover design by Temika Mccanns

Editor and Illustrator: Elsie Bloomfield

Contents

the beginning 4

the struggles..20

the growth 35

the end...55

about the book..74

about the author...75

the beginning

love is a seed, planted deep within,

a feeling that starts to grow and spin.

it sprouts and blossoms, like a flower in bloom,

a light that shines, in a heart's dark room.

it starts as a flutter, a skip in the beat,

a spark in the eye, a smile so sweet.

it's a feeling so pure, so innocent and true,

a love that's just starting, to come into view.

it's the first time you meet, the first time you touch,

the first time you know, that this is it, so much.

it's the first time you laugh, the first time you cry,

the first time you realize, you're not alone, you'll never die.

it's the first time you see, the world in a new light,

the first time you feel, everything is just right.

it's the first time you know, you're not alone,

the first time you realize, you've found your own.

it's the first time you dream, the first time you hope,

the first time you realize, that you can cope.

it's the first time you feel, that you're alive,

the first time you know, that you'll survive.

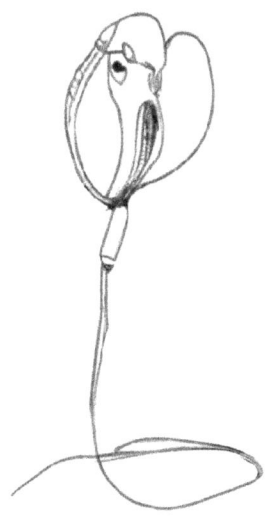

love's beginning is a time of joy,

a time of hope, a brand new boy.

it's a time to cherish, a time to hold,

a time to dream, a time to be bold.

so let love in, let it start,

let it grow and reach your heart.

for love's beginning, is a gift to treasure,

a feeling that will last forever.

tender tulip

love is a breeze, that gently blows,

a feeling that softly glows.

it's a whisper in the night,

a guiding light, that makes everything right.

it starts as a flicker, a flame in the heart,

a spark in the soul, a new work of art.

it's a feeling so pure, so true and divine,

a love that's just starting, to make you shine.

it's the first touch of hands, the first kiss on lips,

the first time you know, this is it, no more trips.

it's the first time you laugh, the first time you
cry,

the first time you realize, you're not alone,
you'll never die.

it's the first time you see, the world in a new way,

the first time you feel, everything is okay.

it's the first time you know, you're not alone,

the first time you realize, you've found your own.

it's the first time you dream, the first time you hope,

the first time you realize, that you can cope.

it's the first time you feel, that you're alive,

the first time you know, that you'll survive.

love's beginning is a time of growth,

a time of newness, a brand new hope.

it's a time to cherish, a time to hold,

a time to dream, a time to be bold.

so let love in, let it start,

let it grow and reach your heart.

for love's beginning, is a gift to treasure,

a feeling that will last forever.

love is a spark, a flicker in the dark

a feeling that starts as a timid spark

a dream in the night, a hope in the day

a light that shines, in a heart's darkest way

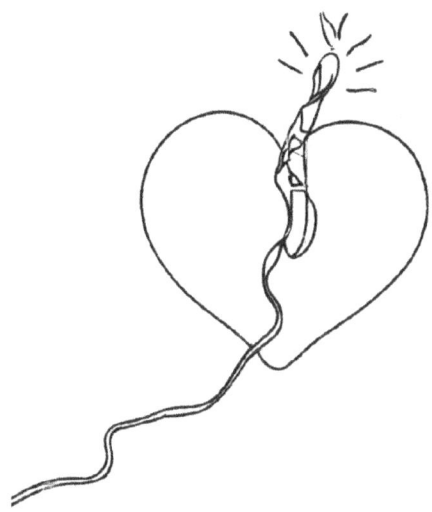

it starts with a glance, a smile, a touch

a feeling that's pure, that means so much

a heart that beats, a spirit that sings

a love that's just starting, it blossoms and brings

it's the first time you meet, the first time you laugh

the first time you know, this love is not a gaffe

it's the first time you dream, the first time you hope

the first time you realize, this love is not a trope

it's the first time you see, the world in a new light

the first time you feel, everything is just right

it's the first time you know, you're not alone

the first time you realize, you've found your own home

the struggles

love is a battle, fought with each heart,

a feeling that tears us apart.

it's a war between what's right and wrong,

a fight to hold on, to what we've begun.

it starts as a struggle, a test of our will,

a challenge of trust, a test of our thrill.

it's a feeling so fragile, so easy to lose,

a love that's on the line, we're left to choose.

it's the first time you doubt, the first time you fear,

the first time you know, this love is not sincere.

it's the first time you cry, the first time you scream,

the first time you realize, love's not as it seems.

it's the first time you see, the cracks in the facade,

the first time you feel, love has betrayed you and all.

it's the first time you know, you're not alone,

the first time you realize, you've lost your own.

it's the first time you grieve, the first time you ache,

the first time you realize, love's mistake.

it's the first time you feel, that you're alive,

the first time you know, that you'll survive.

love's struggles are a test of our strength,

a test of our perseverance, at any length.

it's a time to reflect, a time to heal,

a time to learn, a time to feel.

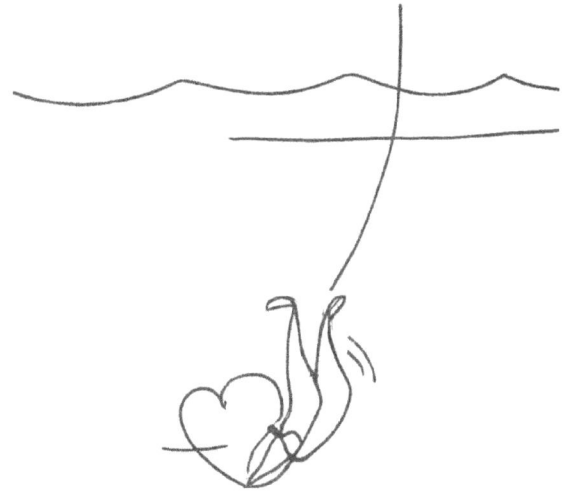

love is a storm, that rages inside,

a feeling that makes us collide.

it's a tempest, that shakes us to the core,

a fight to stand tall, and weather the storm.

it starts as a struggle, a test of our heart,

a battle of emotions, a test of our part.

it's a feeling so fragile, so hard to sustain,

a love that's on the line, that causes pain.

it's the first time you question, the first time you doubt,

the first time you know, this love is what it's about.

it's the first time you yell, the first time you cry,

the first time you realize, love's not a easy ride.

it's the first time you see, the other side,

the first time you feel, love's not a one-sided tide.

it's the first time you know, you're not alone,

the first time you realize, you both have grown.

it's the first time you forgive, the first time you move on,

the first time you realize, love's not always a song.

it's the first time you feel, that you're alive,

the first time you know, that you'll survive.

love's struggles are a test of our patience,

a test of our resilience, in every instance.

it's a time to learn, a time to grow,

a time to evolve, and let love flow.

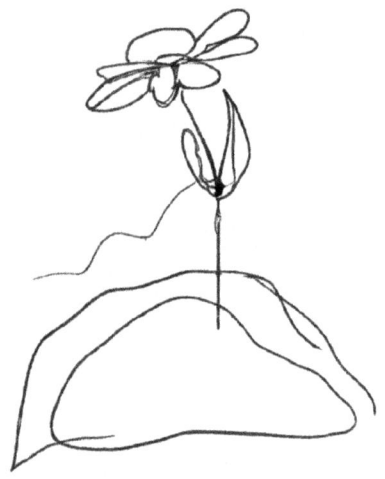

so let love struggle, let it test,

let it make us stronger, let it be the best.

for love's struggles, are a part of the journey,

a feeling that will make us strong and merry.

love is a storm

that rages inside

a feeling that makes us collide

it's a tempest

that shakes us to the core

a fight to stand tall

and weather the storm

it starts as a struggle

a test of our hearts

a battle of emotions

a test of our parts

it's a feeling so fragile

so hard to sustain

a love that's on the line

that causes pain

it's the first time we question

the first time we doubt

the first time we know

this love is what it's about

it's the first time we yell

the first time we cry

the first time we realize

love's not a easy ride

love's struggles are a test

of our patience and trust

a time to learn and grow

a time to evolve and trust

so let love struggle

let it test

let it make us stronger

let it be the best

for love's struggles

are a part of the journey

a feeling that will make us strong and merry

the growth

love is a seed, nurtured with care,

a feeling that blossoms, with time to spare.

it's a garden, that grows with each passing day,

a beauty, that never fades away.

it starts as a sprout, fragile and small,

a promise of growth, that stands tall.

it's a feeling so pure, so worth the wait,

a love that's worth fighting for, it's never too late.

tender tulip

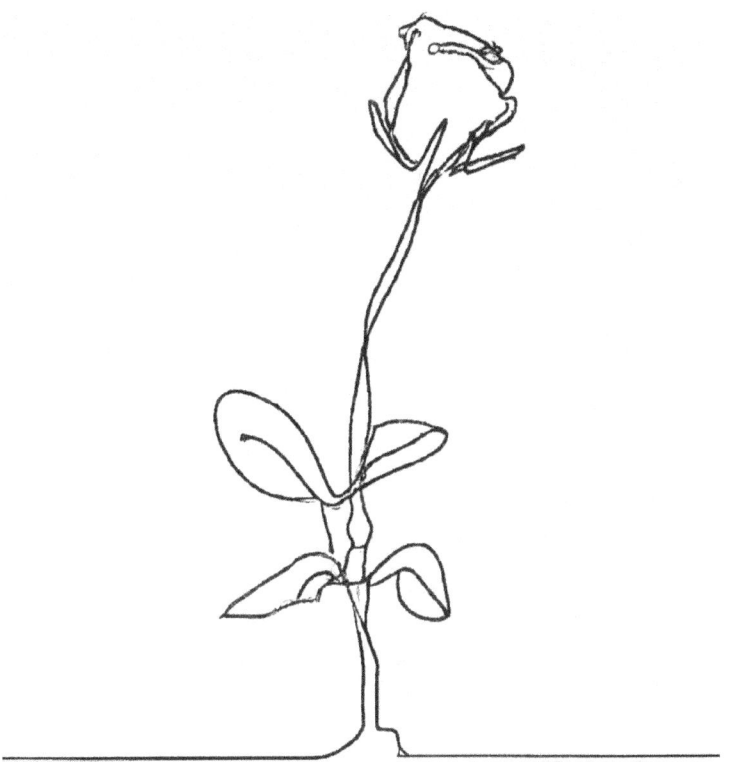

it's the first time you heal, the first time you trust,

the first time you know, love is a must.

it's the first time you laugh, the first time you smile,

the first time you realize, love's worth the while.

it's the first time you see, the beauty in change,

the first time you feel, love's not a thing to arrange.

it's the first time you know, you're not alone,

the first time you realize, you've found your own.

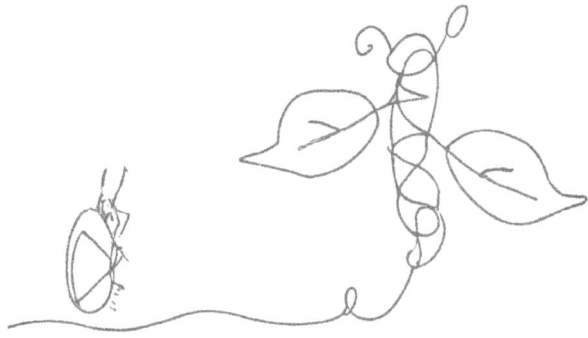

it's the first time you forgive, the first time you let go,

the first time you realize, love's a constant flow.

it's the first time you feel, that you're alive,

the first time you know, that you'll survive.

love's growth is a journey, of self-discovery,

a journey of healing, of love's recovery.

it's a time to learn, a time to grow,

a time to evolve, and let love flow.

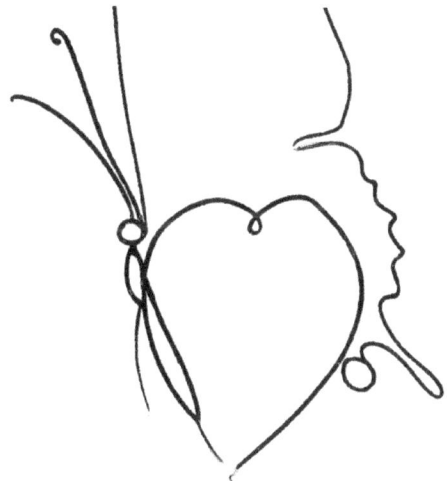

it's a time to let go, of past hurt and pain,

a time to forgive, and start again.

it's a time to open up, to a new love's start,

a time to heal, and mend a broken heart.

love is a rose, that blooms with time,

a feeling that shines, in every rhyme.

it's a garden, that grows with each passing day,

a beauty, that never fades away.

it starts as a sprout, fragile and small,

a promise of growth, that stands tall.

it's a feeling so pure, so worth the wait,

a love that's worth fighting for, it's never too late.

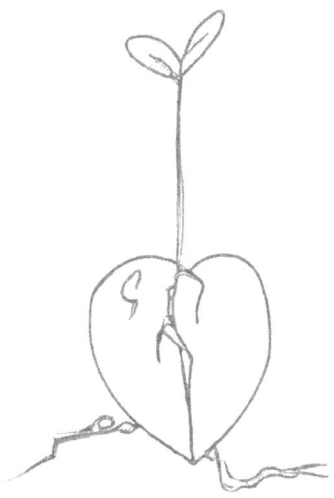

it's the first time you learn, the first time you grow,

the first time you know, love's a constant flow.

it's the first time you laugh, the first time you smile,

the first time you realize, love's worth the while.

it's the first time you see, the beauty in change,

the first time you feel, love's not a thing to arrange.

it's the first time you know, you're not alone,

the first time you realize, you've found your own.

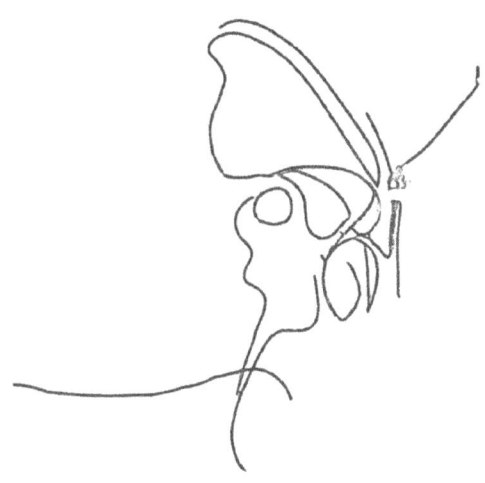

it's the first time you forgive, the first time you let go,

the first time you realize, love's a ebb and flow.

it's the first time you feel, that you're alive,

the first time you know, that you'll survive.

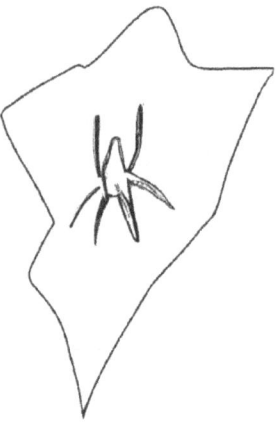

love's growth is a journey, of self-discovery,

a journey of healing, of love's recovery.

it's a time to let go, of past hurt and pain,

a time to forgive, and start again.

it's a time to open up, to a new love's start,

a time to heal, and mend a broken heart.

it's a time to learn, to love oneself,

a time to grow, to be proud and be oneself.

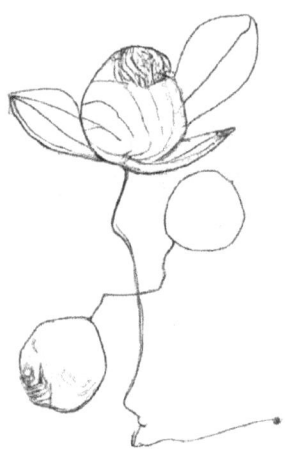

it's a time to learn, to trust and to share,

a time to grow, to be strong and to care.

for love's growth, is a gift to treasure,

a feeling that will last forever.

love is a seed

nurtured with care

a feeling that blossoms

with time to spare

it's a garden

that grows with each passing day

a beauty that never fades away

it starts as a sprout

fragile and small

a promise of growth

that stands tall

it's a feeling so pure

so worth the wait

a love that's worth fighting for

it's never too late

it's the first time we heal

the first time we trust

the first time we know

love is a must

it's the first time we laugh

the first time we smile

the first time we realize

love's worth the while

it's the first time we see

the beauty in change

the first time we feel

love's not a thing to arrange

it's the first time we know

we're not alone

the first time we realize

we've found our own

love's growth is a journey

of self-discovery

a journey of healing

of love's recovery

it's a time to learn

a time to grow

a time to evolve

and let love flow

for love's growth

is a gift to treasure

a feeling that will last forever

the end

love is a sunset, that fades into night,

a feeling that loses its light.

it's a goodbye, that's said with a tear,

a memory, that's left to hold dear.

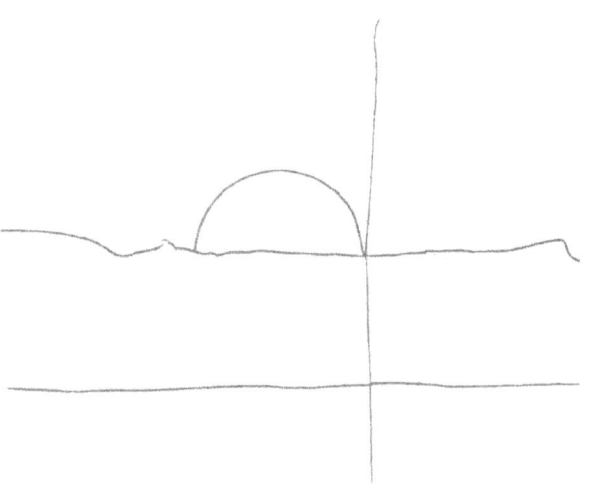

it starts as a closure, a final goodbye,

a last chance to try, to make love fly.

it's a feeling so bittersweet, so hard to let go,

a love that's ended, to make room for the new.

it's the first time you say, the first time you part,

the first time you know, this love is not smart.

it's the first time you cry, the first time you sigh,

the first time you realize, love's time has gone
by.

it's the first time you see, the end in sight,

the first time you feel, love's fading light.

it's the first time you know, you're not alone,

the first time you realize, you'll find your own.

it's the first time you grieve, the first time you ache,

the first time you realize, love's time to break.

it's the first time you feel, that you're alive,

the first time you know, that you'll survive.

love's end is a journey, of self-discovery,

a journey of healing, of love's recovery.

it's a time to let go, of past hurt and pain,

a time to forgive, and start again.

it's a time to open up, to a new love's start,

a time to heal, and mend a broken heart.

it's a time to learn, to love oneself,

a time to grow, to be proud and be oneself.

it's a time to learn, to trust and to share,

a time to grow, to be strong and to care.

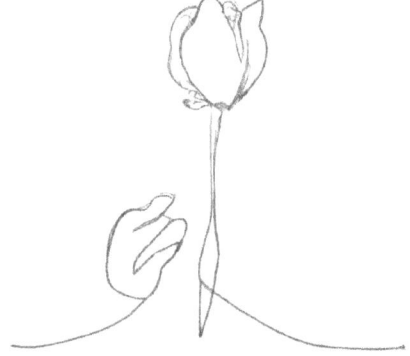

it's a time to remember, the love that's passed,

a time to cherish, the love that's last.

it's a time to accept, love's final stage,

a time to move on, and turn the page.

love's end is a lesson, in life's great plan,

a reminder, that love will come again.

it's a time to grieve, and then to heal,

a time to love again, and make it real.

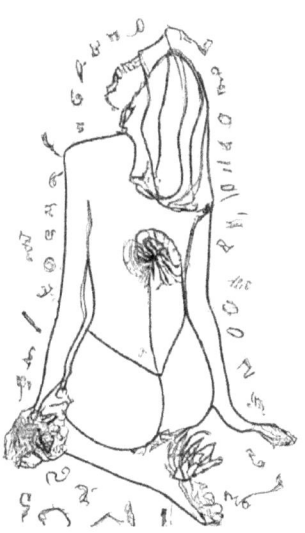

for love's end, is not the end at all,

it's a new beginning, a new love call.

it's a time to trust, in love once more,

a time to open up, and let love soar.

so let love end, let it go,

let it make way, for a love that's new and aglow.

for love's end, is a part of the journey,

a feeling that will lead to new love's glory.

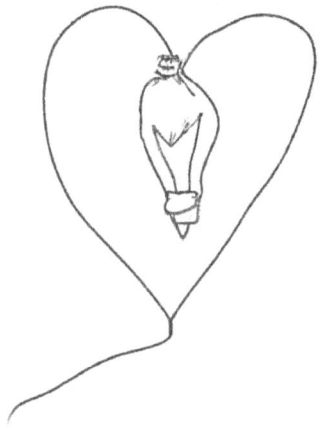

love is a sunset

that fades into night

a feeling that loses its light

it's a goodbye

said with a tear

a memory left to hold dear

it starts as a closure

a final goodbye

a last chance to try

to make love fly

it's a feeling so bittersweet

so hard to let go

a love that's ended

to make room for the new

it's the first time we say goodbye

the first time we part

the first time we know

this love is not smart

it's the first time we cry

the first time we sigh

the first time we realize

love's time has gone by

love's end is a journey

of self-discovery

a journey of healing

of love's recovery

it's a time to let go

of past hurt and pain

a time to forgive

and start again

it's a time to open up

to a new love's start

a time to heal

and mend a broken heart

it's a time to learn

to love oneself

a time to grow

to be proud and be oneself

for love's end

is not the end at all

it's a new beginning

a new love call

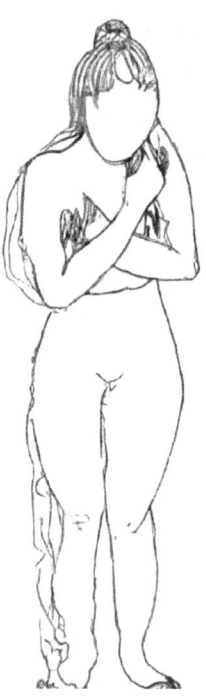

about the book

"It starts with us" is a collection of poetry about love,

A story of growth, a tale from above.

A journey of self-discovery,

Of trust and heartbreak, and love's recovery.

Through laughter and tears, we see characters grow,

As they learn to let go, and to let love flow.

A story of hope, in the face of despair,

Of finding oneself, and learning to care.

A tale of love, that will stay with you,

A journey worth taking, a story true.

"It starts with us" a Poetry to treasure,

A love to remember, forever and ever.

about the author

Amsterdam-born poet Tender Tulip has garnered international acclaim for her work. at the university of Amsterdam, she majored in literature and creative writing after being moved to do so by the works of Dutch poets. her first poetry collection, "it starts with us," was hailed by critics and helped launch her career as a prominent poet. her poetry is renowned for its ability to depict the intricacies of human relationships with a raw emotional intensity. tender tulip is still a resident of Amsterdam, and her poetry has appeared in numerous publications.

www.ingramcontent.com/pod-product-compliance
Lightning Source LLC
Chambersburg PA
CBHW070933120626
46546CB00004B/1409